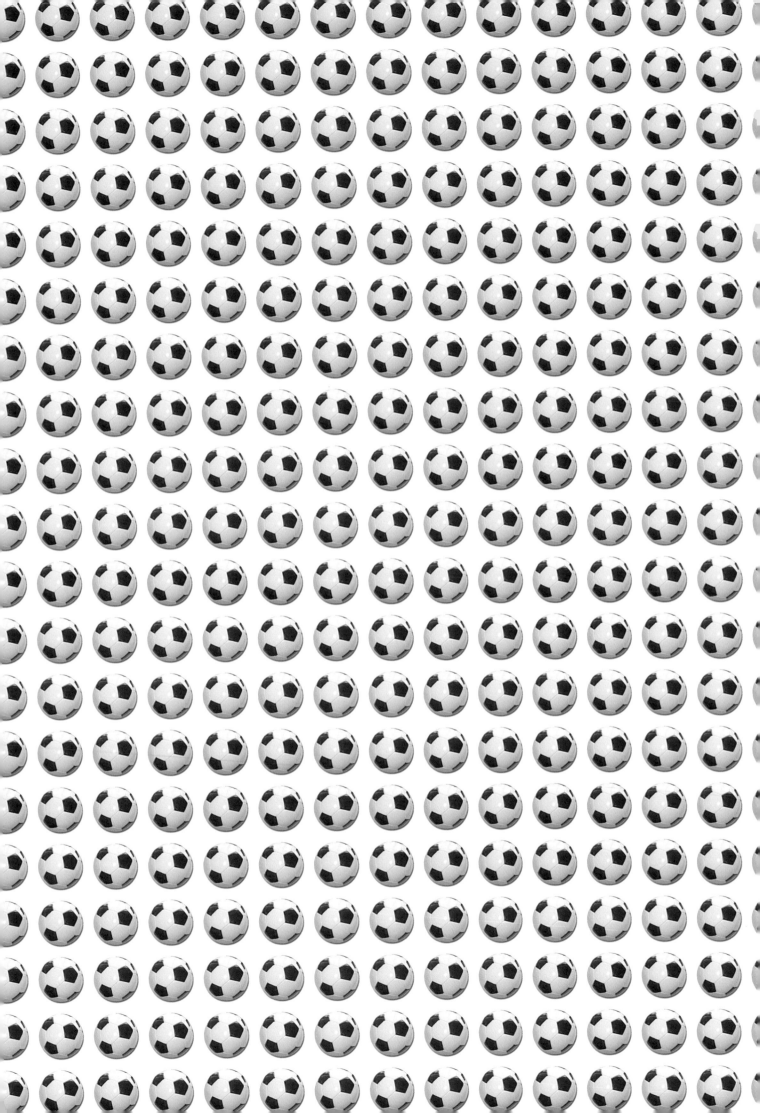

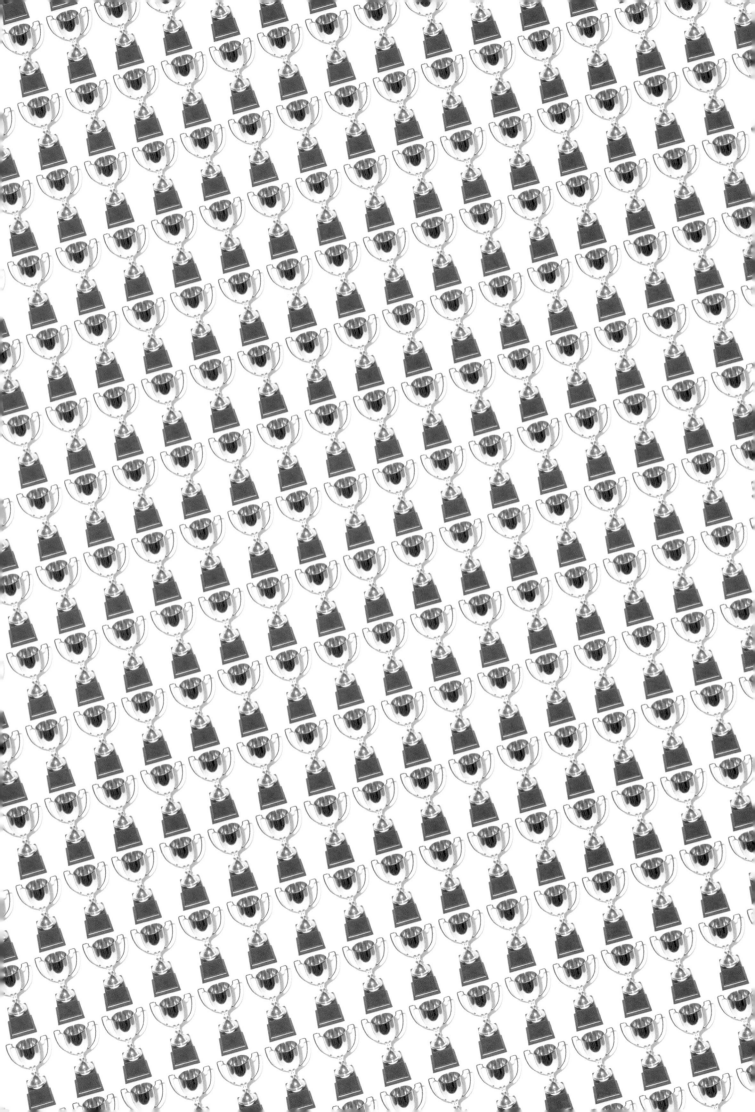

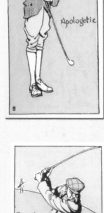

HAMMOND
(GLOUCESTERSHIRE)

P. HOLMES. YORKSHIRE

C. HALLOWS
(LANCASHIRE)

Mr. J. M. GREGORY
N.S.W. AUSTRALIA

T. W. GODDARD
(GLOUCESTERSHIRE)

G. GUNN. NOTTS

PLAYER'S CIGARETTES

G. GEARY
(LEICESTERSHIRE)

PLAYER'S CIGARETTES

C. W. L. PARKER
GLOUCESTERSHIRE

PLAYER'S CIGARETTES

A. H. H. GILLIGAN (SUSSEX)

PLAYER'S CIGARETTES

W. R. HAMMOND
(GLOUCESTERSHIRE)

PLAYER'S CIGARETTES

P. HOLMES. YORKSHIRE

PLAYER'S CIGARETTES

C. HALLOWS
(LANCASHIRE)

PLAYER'S CIGARETTES

J. M. GREGORY
N.S.W. AUSTRALIA

PLAYER'S CIGARETTES

T. W. GODDARD
(GLOUCESTERSHIRE)

PLAYER'S CIGARETTES

G. GUNN. NOTTS

PLAYER'S CIGARETTES

G. GEARY
(LEICESTERSHIRE)

PLAYER'S CIGARETTES

C. W. L. PARKER
GLOUCESTERSHIRE

PLAYER'S CIGARETTES

A. H. H. GILLIGAN (SUSSEX)

PLAYER'S CIGARETTES

R. HAMMOND
(GLOUCESTERSHIRE)

PLAYER'S CIGARETTES

P. HOLMES. YORKSHIRE

PLAYER'S CIGARETTES

C. HALLOWS
(LANCASHIRE)

PLAYER'S CIGARETTES

Mr. J. M. GREGORY
N.S.W. AUSTRALIA

PLAYER'S CIGARETTES

T. W. GODDARD
(GLOUCESTERSHIRE)

PLAYER'S CIGARETTES

G. GUNN. NOTTS

PLAYER'S CIGARETTES

PLAYER'S CIGARETTES

PLAYER'S CIGARETTES

PLAYER'S CIGARETTES